The Adventures of Max & Liz
Book 1

The Secret Shed

by Cheryl Orlassino

Blast Off to Learning Press

**Visit our site for the comprehension PDF
that accompanies this book.**

www.BlastOffToLearningPress.com

Published by
Blast Off to Learning Press
New York

Copyright © 2021 All rights reserved.

e-mail all inquiries to:
contact@BlastOffToLearningPress.com

Printed in the United States of America
ISBN: 978-0-9831996-5-6

Attention Parents!

If your child is in need of reading help, check out our *Blast Off to Reading* program.

This reading program includes a workbook with step-by-step lessons, as well as online tools and games that your child will love.

We also have a reading program for little ones!

✓ No Training Needed

✓ Step by Step

✓ Scripted Lessons

✓ Multisensory

✓ Engaging Games

For Elizabeth & Christopher,
whose adventures inspired this story.

Chapter 1

A Spring Day

It was a spring day. The first spring day that was not cold. I sat on the bus thinking. I wanted to ride my bike in the woods. I was stuck inside all winter, and it was time to go out. My bike was new, and I couldn't wait to ride it.

My bus made a turn. I could see Jack's house. Jack would be home. He was in sixth grade and in middle school. The middle school kids get home before we do. I smiled to myself. I'll text Jack as soon as I get home.

"Hi Max!" my mom said, as I walked in the house. "How was your day?"

"Hi," I said. "Good." I put my backpack on the table. "I want to go out and ride my bike with

Jack."

My mom made a face. "First do your homework," she said. "You have a game after dinner. You won't have time to do your work."

I sat down at the kitchen table and took my phone out of my bag. As I sent a text to Jack, my mom put a snack in in front of me.

Bike in woods?

"Homework," she said.

I took my books out of my bag. "I will," I said. "I have one math sheet."

While I did my math, my phone made a chime sound. Jack texted me back. He wanted to meet me on the corner. That is the half-way spot between his house and my house.

I put my paper back in my bag and put on my jacket.

"I'm going out!" I yelled. I got my bike out of the garage and rode it down the street. I didn't see Jack on the corner. Jack was late. He was always late.

I got to the corner and got off my bike. Mr. Upton was raking his garden. His house is right on the corner.

"Hi Max," he said. "Nice day to ride a bike."

I nodded.

"Just watch out for cars," he said.

"Oh, we will be in the woods," I said. I pointed down the block to where the woods are.

Mr. Upton smiled. "That sounds like a lot of fun."

Then I saw Jack. "Hey!" I called out.

"Sorry I'm late," Jack said. He waved at Mr. Upton.

"Have fun, boys," Mr. Upton said. "Don't get lost in the woods!"

He was joking with us. The woods were not that big. But

they were big enough to think they were. When you are in the woods, you can't see any houses. You feel like you're far away.

I waved to Mr. Upton and off we went.

Chapter 2

The Woods

We never rode our bikes in the woods before. We only walked around in there with my sister and our dog. But now it was just me and Jack on our bikes. We could explore a lot of the woods. We could go deep and see more.

"Let's go fast!" yelled Jack.

He leaned down on his bike and pumped his feet to speed up. I did the same thing. I was right behind Jack.

There are a lot of paths in the woods. Some paths are wide, and some are not wide at all. The path we were on was wide, so I could pass Jack if I went faster.

Jack turned his head and saw me. "Oh no you don't!" he

said and pumped faster.

Jack was older than me, and he was stronger too. I could not catch up and pass him.

"Wait up!" I yelled when Jack was too far away.

I could see him stop to wait for me.

"Let's go this way," he said when I got close. He pointed to a path that was wide enough for one bike at a time.

I followed again behind Jack. But now Jack went slowly. We had to duck under branches and go over bumpy roots from the trees.

I looked up and saw something in a tree. "Hey, what's that?"

We both stopped riding our bikes and looked up. It was a tree-house from a long time ago. Jack jumped off his bike and ran around the tree. "No ladder," he said, frowning.

I was glad because it didn't look safe. "Come on," I said. "Let's keep going."

Now I was in front, and Jack was behind me. There was a fork in the path, and I chose to go left.

"Hey, look at that!" I said. I slowed down so Jack could get close to see.

There was a big space with no trees or bushes. It was all dirt. But the dirt was carved into deep paths that made twists and turns. Some of the dirt paths led to big mounds of dirt.

"It's a dirt-bike course!" said Jack.

"For bikes?" I asked.

"It's to ride on with a dirt-bike, Max." Jack sounded a bit mad, like I wasn't smart. He pointed to the mounds of dirt. "That's a ramp. If you go fast, you can get up in the air, and do tricks."

"But then you have to land," I said. I was hoping that Jack wouldn't try this. I had my phone to call for help, but I didn't think it would work out in the woods.

We were on a hill and the course was under us. Jack looked down. "This is the start of the course," he said. "You go down this hill to get speed."

Jack hopped on his bike and down he went. He did pick up speed. He went around the first turn fast. He was almost sideways. Then he went over the first bump, went up in the air and landed.

He stopped and looked back at me.

"Try it!" he yelled.

I bit my lip thinking. This bike is new, and I just got it. I was not good at riding it yet. But it did look like fun.

Without thinking more, I pointed my bike down the hill and off I went.

My bike went fast, gaining speed. I pumped my legs making my bike go even faster.

The turn came and I went left, leaning deep. Then I went

over the first bump and was in the air.

"Wow," I said when I landed. "That was so cool."

Jack smiled at me. He didn't think I would do it.

"I wonder who made this," I said as I looked around. "Do you think kids still come back here?"

"Well, the rain would wash it away at some point," he said. "I think someone must still use it."

I nodded. That made sense. I hope they don't mind us using it.

We rode our bikes around the course for a while. But then we left the course behind and went deeper into the woods.

Chapter 3

A New Friend

When the paths were too over-grown, we had to leave our bikes and walk.

"Don't touch any leaves," Jack said. "They could be poison."

I remembered when my dad got poison ivy. He was cleaning

out our garden. He was red and itchy for a week. He was not happy.

"I know," I said looking back at him.

"Watch out for bears," Jack said.

"There are no bears where we live," I said. I think Jack was joking.

"Watch out for spiders," he said.

Sometimes Jack thinks I'm just a ten-year-old kid, and he likes to make fun of me. So what if I'm afraid of spiders? A lot of people are. I wish I never told Jack that.

"Watch out for bats," I said.

"There are no bats around here," he said.

Then I told him about the story of the bat and the girl.

A year ago, a bat got into my school and went into the girls' bathroom. There was a first-grade girl in the bathroom, and she ran out screaming. It was a big story that made the news. If a bat bites you, you can get very sick. The girl had to see a doctor to make sure she was okay.

"Well, they come out at night," he said. "It's daytime."

As I was thinking about bats, I looked to my left and saw a soft brown face. It was a deer. He was about five feet away, just behind a bush. I stopped walking.

"Shh," I said, turning back to Jack. I pointed at the deer. Jack stopped walking too.

The deer had big brown eyes that were looking at me. As he watched me, he ate leaves. Chomp. Chomp. Chomp.

Jack made a face. It was a quiet way to say, "Wow!"

We stood there looking at him. I knew the deer was a 'him' because he had little buds on top of his head. Those will grow to be antlers.

I don't think the deer was

scared. He just chewed and chewed. But he didn't take his eyes off us. We didn't take our eyes off him either. If the deer could talk, he would say, "What are you looking at?"

Then he turned and dashed away. He was fast and very quiet. He was gone in less than a second.

"Max," Jack said, "that was cool."

I nodded. Going into the woods was a lot of fun.

Chapter 4

The Shed

We walked along the paths. I was in front and Jack was in back.

As we walked, I played a joke on Jack. I pulled a branch back. I let it go and it snapped back, hitting Jack on his left arm.

"Ouch, stop that," Jack yelled.

I smiled. I'm not such a little kid now, am I?

We turned one way and then another. With a rock, Jack marked our way on the bark of trees. If you rub a hard rock on  the bark, it makes a light line. If we forget how to get back, we can find the lines.

We were in the woods deep. We were far from any house. It felt like the middle of nowhere.

Then we saw it.

It was old. Very old. Was it a house? Or a barn?

"I think it is an old shed," said Jack.

"Who owns it?" I asked.

Jack shook his head. "They are long gone."

We went closer for a look. Big tree branches hung over it. Bushes pressed into it. It was hidden.

"This is cool," said Jack as he walked up to it.

"Think we can get in?" I asked.

Jack walked up to the old door. It was made of wood. It had lots of cracks in it. Jack pushed it open.

"Wow," he said. The door scraped along the old floor. It did not open all the way.

"It's blocked," I said looking in.

I squeezed in a bit and then

kicked something out of the way.

Jack pushed the door more. Soon there was room for us to go in.

It was dark and dirty. I took out my phone and put the flashlight on. Jack did the same with his phone.

"Check this out," I said pointing my phone at an old roller with a crank. "I think this is an old thing for washing clothes."

"Yes," said Jack. "You put the clothes in and crank. It squeezes the water out."

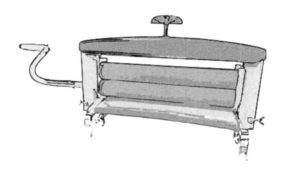

"That must be a hundred years old," I said.

Jack nodded. "My grandma had one from when her mom was a kid. It was in our basement before we moved here."

We took a few steps in and looked around. It was dark and it smelled bad. It smelled like wet dirt and old wood.

"Think this place is haunted?" I asked.

Jack scoffed. "No, but I bet there are a hundred spiders in here."

Spiders!

Just then I felt a soft tickle on my face. A spider-web. Yuck!

I pushed it away and tried not to think of spiders.

We looked around and saw old tools. We saw a wheel-barrow, an axe and garden tools.

My phone made a chime, and I saw that my mom sent a text.

** Dinner soon **

I wanted to stay and see more. But I had to eat dinner and get to the game. There was no time.

"We should head back," I said. "Let's come back tomorrow."

Chapter 5

Another Explorer

I sat at my desk, waiting for the day to end. It was the longest day ever, and I wanted to get home so we could go back to the woods and go back to the shed.

Tick. Tick. Tick. So long.

The sun was out, and it was

warm. It was a perfect spring day.

"Max?" my teacher said.

"Umm," I sat up. Did she call on me?

"Someone has spring fever," she said.

Some of the kids snickered.

"Max," she said, "I'll ask

again. What is the longest day of the year?"

I wanted to say that it was this one, but she

would get mad. Then I had to think. Every day has the same number of hours.

"Umm, is this a trick question?" I asked.

Her lips pressed together. She was getting mad.

"Don't all days have 24 hours?" I asked. I slid down a bit in my chair.

The class joined in. Some kids nodded and some shouted,

"Yes, he's right!"

Mrs. Brix shook her head. "Class!" she yelled. She gave me the side eye. "I mean, what day has the most *day-light*?"

Emma Erickson raised her hand. "I know, I know!" she said.

Mrs. Brix pointed at Emma.

"It is June 20th. That's the first day of summer." She smiled a big smile. "I know that because that's my birthday."

The first day of summer. I could spend all day in those woods. Exploring.

"That's right, Emma." My teacher smiled. "Class, the bell will ring soon. Your homework is to write something about spring and summer. It can be about any topic. I want a full page, nice and neat! This is due tomorrow."

A boy named Ricky raised his hand. "Mrs. Brix," he said. "Can it be about sports?"

"Yes, Ricky. It can be about anything. As long as it has to do with spring and summer."

Just then the bell rang. Time to go home!

* * *

The bus ride seemed longer than normal. I kept thinking about the shed in the woods.

When I opened the door, my sister, Liz, was sitting at the

kitchen table. She was doing homework and eating an apple.

Liz is in the same grade as Jack. They were in the same class when they were five years old. Liz said that Jack was loud in the class and drove the teacher nuts.

When Liz is bored, she will hang out with us. But she is on a dance team and is always busy with that.

"Liz," I said. "Me and Jack

found a cool old shed in the woods."

My mom yelled from the den, "Jack and I." She always tried to fix the way I say things. Me and Jack or Jack and I. What is the big deal?

Liz sat up. She liked the woods.

"Where?" she asked.

"I don't know," I said. It's not like I had a map. "We passed by an old tree-house. And then we passed by a dirt-bike course."

Liz nodded. "Me and Ally, I mean, *Ally and I* rode bikes on that. It was fun. But then Ally found a tick on her neck and now she won't go near the woods."

My mom called from the den. "Kids, if you go into the woods, do a tick check when you come home."

A tick check? Yuck!

"Better yet," my mom said, walking into the kitchen, "I'll do it."

Ticks are a problem here and they can make you sick. We always check our dog for ticks.

"Well," I said, "after the dirt-bike course you have to keep going. Me and Jack, I mean...*Jack and I*... are going back today. Do you want to come?"

Liz chucked her apple core

into the trash. "Do ducks have webbed feet?"

Yes

Chapter 6

Trouble!

Soon the three of us - me, Liz and Jack, were on our bikes, riding in the woods.

We stopped at the dirt-bike course so we could have some fun. My mom calls Liz her "dare devil" because Liz will try anything.

I watched as Liz rode down the big hill, into the deep dirt paths. She turned and went over ramps and landed. Jack was right behind her.

If Liz fell and got hurt, she would not be able to dance. I held my breath. But she didn't fall. I was glad. If Liz got hurt my mom might tell us not to go in the woods.

Now it was my turn. I raced down the hill and took the turns.

I went over a few ramps and landed. It was a lot of fun. But now my new bike had dirt all over it. It was worth it.

We did that for a long time until we were tired. Then we rode on.

We went deeper into the woods. I told Liz about the deer we saw. Liz loves animals more than anything.

"I want to see him," said Liz.

She looked around, but there were no deer to be seen.

When the paths got too small, we had to leave our bikes and walk. Jack led the way.

Soon we came to the shed.

"Awesome," said Liz.

Jack pushed the door open with his foot.   He had his phone light on and went in first.

"Liz," Jack called. "Come in!"

Liz went in, got her phone out and put her flashlight on. She aimed the light all around. "Wow," she said. "What is all this stuff?"

I was behind her. "Old stuff," I said. "Like 100 years old."

"A lot of tools," she said. "This was a tool shed."

"And other stuff too," said Jack.

From far off I heard a motor

make a loud sound. What was that? I stuck my head outside.

The sound was getting louder.

Was it a car, or a lawn mower? The sound grew louder and louder. Then it sounded like more than one.

I stepped out of the shed and looked around to the back.

Then I saw them!

I jumped into the shed and pulled the door shut.

"Quads!" I said.

Quads are what the big kids had. They have four wheels, and they make a lot of noise. They are also fast. Very fast. The kids ride them up and down our street.

But now they're in the woods.

Now I knew why there were paths that were so wide in the woods. Those were from the quads.

The big kids yelled to each other. I could not make out what they said. Did they find our bikes?

"The bikes," I said. I just got mine, it was new, and it was laying on the ground with Liz's bike and Jack's bike.

"Shh," said Liz.

"But they might find them," I said.

"No," said Jack. "The bikes are on the small paths and the quads will stay on the wide paths."

True. I didn't think of that.

The quads' sound got lower and lower until we could hardly hear them.

"I think they're gone," said Jack.

"I think we should go," I said. I wanted to check on my bike.

"But I want to look more," said Liz.

Jack said, "We can always come back. Besides, my dad is picking me up soon."

"Fine," Liz said as she rolled her eyes at us.

We shut the shed door all the way. Then Liz found a big branch that was laying on the ground. She dragged it to the shed and laid it in front of the shed's door.

"This will help hide the shed," she said.

We looked around. There was no sound. It was quiet.

"Let's go," said Jack.

We walked to our bikes. The

bikes were fine. The quads didn't run over them.

We rode on the little paths, in a line. Jack was first, then Liz, and then me.

Soon we were on a big path. I rode next to Jack and Liz was in front.

"Watch out, Max," Liz said looking back at me. "The quads are going to get you!"

And just like that, we heard

quad motors. They were far away but getting louder.

"Thanks, Liz!" I hissed at her.

She turned and frowned at me. "I didn't make them come back!"

The sound got louder and louder. VROOM! VROOM!

I looked back and saw them coming at us.

"Guys! They're coming!" I

yelled.

We pumped our legs and went as fast as we could go. The sound got louder. They were getting closer.

What were they going to do? Run us over?

Jack yelled, "Let's get off the big path."

We turned and went down the first small path we could find.

One after the other; Liz, Jack and then me.

When we were far away from the big path, we put our bikes on the ground. Then we hid behind a big tree.

We waited as the sound got louder and louder. Then the sound got lower. Lower. Lower. Then we knew they were far away. We were safe.

"That was close," said Jack.

Liz nodded.

We went back to our bikes and headed home.

Chapter 7

The Story

That night, I sat at the kitchen table. I told my mom that for homework I needed to write about spring and summer.

"What about flowers?" she said. "Or write about the bees."

I shook my head. Flowers and bees are boring.

Liz sipped her drink, thinking. "I know," she said. She reached into the back pocket of her jeans. She took out a folded paper and tossed it to me. It landed on the table.

"What's this?" I asked as I picked it up.

It was part of an old newspaper page. It was yellow

and faded.

"I found it in the shed," said Liz. "It was in a box. The box had a lot of old papers and old books."

"I didn't see that," I said.

Liz sipped her drink. "You rushed us out when the quads came," she said. "I

grabbed the first thing I could and put it in my pocket."

I frowned and looked at the paper. "What does this have to do with spring and summer?" I asked.

Liz made a face at me. "It has stuff about farming. Just read it."

The newspaper was old and in bad shape. It felt damp. I unfolded it slowly so it wouldn't fall apart.

The top had big black letters that said "**The New Village Sentinel**". Under that it said the date, "Saturday, April 8, 1916".

Jack and I were right. That was over 100 years ago! The shed was very old.

There were ads for old stuff all over the page. And there was a small article at the bottom, on the left side.

The *Plowing Starts*

After a harsh winter, farmers are planting. Mr. James Hobbs of New Village, one of our colored farmers, plans to plow and plant

I couldn't read any more.

The ink was a big smear, and the paper was ripped.

"Mom," I asked, "what is a colored farmer?"

My mom set her tea-cup down. "Well, in the old days they used the word 'colored' for African Americans."

"So, the farmer was black?" I asked.

She took the paper from me and read it. "Yes, where did you

get this?"

Liz spoke. "From an old shed in the woods."

My mom nodded. "This is about the farm across the street," she said. "The farmer was a black man named Hobbs."

"But the year is 1916," I said. "That's over 100 years ago."

My mom sat down and opened her laptop and started looking.

"Yes," she said. "James Hobbs came here from the south in 1906. He worked on the farm. Then he bought it. It was his farm."

"That must be his shed," said Liz.

The farm is right across the street from my house. Every day I wake up and look out my window to see the farm. There are always farm people there. Even when the sun is hardly up.

The farm is not very big, and we don't live in a place that has a lot of farms. That is why we live in a cool place. We also have more woods around than other places. We are very lucky to grow up here.

"You should show that clipping to the farm people," my mother said. "They would like that."

***

The next day, after school, I rode my bike to the point of the farm. The land is shaped like a slice of pizza, and the pointy part is where the farm-house is. Jack came with me. Liz had to go to dance class.

A lady waved her hand. "Hi there," she said. "Did you come to help out?"

We got off our bikes, and I took the old paper out of my pocket and said, "We found this story about the old farmer." I held the paper out and pointed to the part that had the story.

She took it and read it. "This

is wonderful," she said. "That's why the farm is called Bethel-Hobbs Community Farm."

"Who is Bethel?" I asked.

"Oh, well," she said. "After James Hobbs died in 1929 his son Alfred took over. He didn't have kids. When he died, he left the farm to his church. The church was an African American church called Bethel AME."

"Oh," I said.

"And now it's a community farm," she said. "That means we all run it. And we give the food we grow to the poor."

I smiled. "I bet Mr. Hobbs would like that."

"And any time you want to help out, come on over!"

Chapter 8

Back to the Shed

My teacher, Mrs. Brix, liked my paper about Hobbs farm. She liked it because it was real, and I had a newspaper clipping about it that was very old.

I wrote about what farmers do in the spring. How they plow and get the dirt ready for planting. Then I wrote about how they plant seeds and grow plants. By summer, a lot of vegetables are ready to be picked.

Then I wrote about our farm. The farm that is part of our town's history.

"This may be the best paper I have seen," she said. She made a copy of the paper clipping and hung it on the wall.

I didn't tell anyone where

we found the paper. I wanted to keep the shed a secret. I didn't want kids to find it and wreck it. Jack and Liz agreed. It was our secret.

***

It was a few weeks later when we went back to the shed. It rained for a lot of days and we had to wait. Liz had dance class every day to get ready for a show. Jack got in trouble and was grounded for a week.

I wanted to go by myself, but then I remembered the quads and felt I should wait.

Finally, we went back to the woods. We passed the tree-house, the dirt-bike course, and then started walking on the over-grown paths.

"I think we shouldn't take anything out of the shed," I said. "It doesn't belong to us."

"But then someone else can

take it," said Liz.

"Like the quad kids," said Jack.

"No," I said. "They go too fast and would never see the shed."

"You can't be sure," said Liz.

That was true, but I didn't think they would care if they did see the shed. They just wanted to go fast on their quads.

"Do you think the shed belongs to the farm people?" I asked.

"I don't know," said Jack. "The shed is in the woods. The farm is not that close."

That was true, but maybe the Hobbs' land was bigger in the old days. I wondered who owned the woods.

Then we saw the shed. We moved the big branch that was in

front of the door. Then we pushed the door open and went in.

* * *

"There's the box that had the newspaper," said Liz. She pointed her light into the box. "There's more here, but they aren't in good shape."

I went over to look. I put my light on a newspaper. Some of it could be read. Some parts looked like they were wet at one time but were now dry. Other parts were black or torn.

"Wow, this one is about a war," I said.

Jack came over. He took the paper and said, "This is from 1916. This is about World War I."

That's the same year as the paper about farmer Hobbs. He farmed the land during the first world war.

"Wow, that's cool," I said as I looked at some of the old books. "Maybe this stuff should be in the library."

Liz held up an old leather apron. It was stiff like it was frozen. "Or a museum," she said.

"Look," said Jack. "A can filled with old coins!" He shook the can. Clank, clank, clank.

Another box had old bottles. They were all different shapes

and colors. Some were small and brown, others were big and green. Some had labels and some were clear.

Next to the box was a big rusty oil can. Next to that was some kind of machine. And, next to that

was an old wheel with spokes around it.

"Do you think James Hobbs rode that bike?" I asked, as I pointed to an old, rusty bicycle that leaned against the wall.

"Maybe," said Liz. "Or maybe it was his son's bike."

Jack sat down on a wooden crate. "There is so much in here," he said. "The shed is packed."

"Maybe we should tell someone about the shed," said Liz. "This stuff will fall apart soon. And maybe other people would want to see it."

But it was our secret place. If we told people about the shed, then it wouldn't be our secret anymore.

"What do you think, Jack?" I asked.

"Well," he said. "It seems wrong to keep it just for us."

Then Liz said, "One bad storm and all of this may be gone forever."

A bad storm could blow the shed over. There were holes in the roof and the walls didn't seem strong.

"Liz," said Jack, "I think

you're right. This stuff should be at our library."

Liz looked at me. "Max, think about it. Look at the roof. It's only a matter of time."

"Okay," I said. "Let's ask mom to help us."

Chapter 9

The Museum Corner

We have the best library in the country. It has everything.

There is a big room filled with toys for little kids to play. Bigger kids use the computers to play games and do homework. And an old row-boat sits in the middle of the kids' big room.

By the front desk, there is a
big fish tank, filled with all kinds
of fish. The outside has an area
for little kids to explore. And, in
the back of the big room, there is
the Museum Corner.

The Museum Corner is not
just for kids. It is for anyone who
likes history.

Now everyone can see all
the things that people, in our

town, used 100 years ago. They can see the old bike, the wheel-barrow, the old tools, the old laundry dryer, the bottles, the coins and everything else.

A table holds the old books that you can look at. And all the newspapers are behind glass. Anyone can read the articles without ripping the paper.

This is a bit of history about our farm, the only farm left in our town.

"Thanks to these three," Ms. Kelly said, looking at us, "we now have a great treasure for our town."

Ms. Kelly was the lady who put everything in the Museum Corner together. She stood just outside the Museum Corner, with us next to her. There was a yellow ribbon across the way to get in.

A crowd of people watched as she cut the ribbon.

Flashes from cameras went off. Some of the flashes were from reporters. There was also a news crew there. We were going to be on TV!

Now a lot of the stuff from the shed would be safe. And it would also be seen by a lot of people.

We did keep the shed a secret. And it's a good thing too. Because when we got everything out of the shed, we found... a trap door!

The End

About Hobbs Farm

    The Long Island town of Centereach, NY, used to be called West Middle Island, until it was renamed to New Village. In 1916, when a map was being made of New York, it was then discovered that the name "New Village" was already used by a town in upstate New York. Consequently, the town was renamed to its present name, Centereach.

    James Hobbs moved from Georgia to New Village in 1906 with his newborn son, Alfred. James worked on a farm and then purchased land for his own farm. This was historic because James was a black man and not many black people owned land at that time.

When James Hobbs died in 1929, his son Alfred took over. Alfred had only had a fifth-grade education, and his wife (born in 1908) and had an eighth-grade education, which was quite common in those days. They did not have any children, and when they passed away, the farm was left to their church.

Today, the historic farm is known as The Bethel-Hobbs Community Farm. Dedicated volunteers work on the farm to provide produce to local food pantries.

The characters, Max and Liz, are based upon two children who grew up across the street from the farm, and the author often enjoys walking around the 11 acres to get fresh air.

The children, along with their neighborhood friend, did find a shed in the woods while exploring. Having seen many of the items described in this story, the shed was always a mystery that added to their childhoods. There were also quads.

Made in the USA
Columbia, SC
14 March 2021

34452498R00065